Great African-Americans

Jackie
ROBINSON

by Isabel Martin   Consulting Editor: Gail Saunders-Smith, PhD

CAPSTONE PRESS
a capstone imprint

Pebble Books are published by Capstone Press,
1710 Roe Crest Drive, North Mankato, Minnesota 56003
www.capstonepub.com

Library of Congress Cataloging-in-Publication Data
Martin, Isabel, 1977–
  Jackie Robinson / by Isabel Martin.
    pages cm. — (Pebble books. Great African-Americans)
  Includes bibliographical references and index.
  Summary: "Simple text and photographs present the life of Jackie Robinson, the first
African-American to play baseball in the Major Leagues"—Provided by publisher.
  ISBN 978-1-4914-0502-4 (library binding) — ISBN 978-1-4914-0508-6 (pbk.) —
  ISBN 978-1-4914-0514-7 (ebook pdf)
1. Robinson, Jackie, 1919–1972—Juvenile literature. 2. Baseball players—United States—
Biography—Juvenile literature. 3. African American baseball players—Biography—Juvenile
literature. I. Title.
  GV865.R6M38 2015
  796.357092—dc23
  [B]   2013049780

Editorial Credits
Nikki Bruno Clapper, editor; Terri Poburka, designer; Kelly Garvin, media researcher;
Laura Manthe, production specialist

Photo Credits
Corbis/Bettmann, cover, 8, 14, 16, 18; Getty Images Inc.: Getty Images Sport, 4; Hulton
Archive, 6; MLB Photos, 20; Library of Congress, 12; National Baseball Hall of Fame Library, 10;
Shutterstock/RONORMANJR, cover art

Note to Parents and Teachers

The Great African-Americans set supports national curriculum standards for
social studies related to people, places, and environments. This book describes and
illustrates Jackie Robinson. The images support early readers in understanding
the text. The repetition of words and phrases helps early readers learn new words.
This book also introduces early readers to subject-specific vocabulary words, which
are defined in the Glossary section. Early readers may need assistance to read
some words and to use the Table of Contents, Glossary, Read More, Internet Sites,
Critical Thinking Using the Common Core, and Index sections of the book.

Printed in the United States of America in Stevens Point, Wisconsin.
032014   008092WZF14

Table of Contents

Meet Jackie

Jackie Robinson was the first African-American in Major League Baseball. Jackie showed that black and white people could work together.

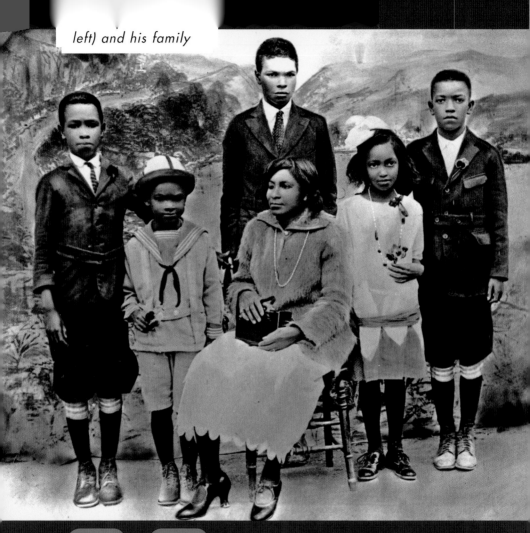

1919

born

1920

moves to
California

Young Jackie

Jackie was born in Georgia in 1919. His mother raised five children by herself. Jackie's family moved to California in 1920.

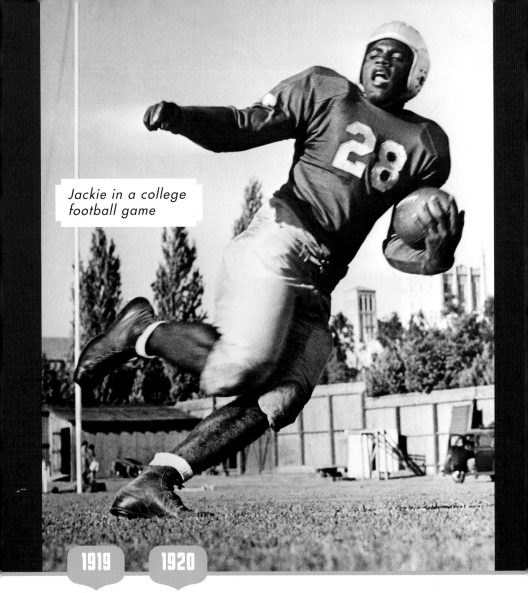

Jackie in a college football game

1919
born

1920
moves to California

Jackie was a sports star

in high school and college.

He was in football, basketball,

baseball, and track and field.

Jackie left college to earn

money for his family.

Jackie as a soldier

1919 born

1920 moves to California

1942 joins U.S. Army

As a Grown-Up

Jackie joined the U.S. Army
in 1942. Some soldiers
treated him poorly because
he was African-American.
But Jackie worked hard
at his job anyway.

| 1919 | 1920 | 1942 | 1945 |
| born | moves to California | joins U.S. Army | joins Kansas City Monarchs |

In 1945 Jackie joined the

Kansas City Monarchs.

This team was in a baseball

league for only blacks.

African-Americans were not

allowed on Major League

Baseball teams at the time.

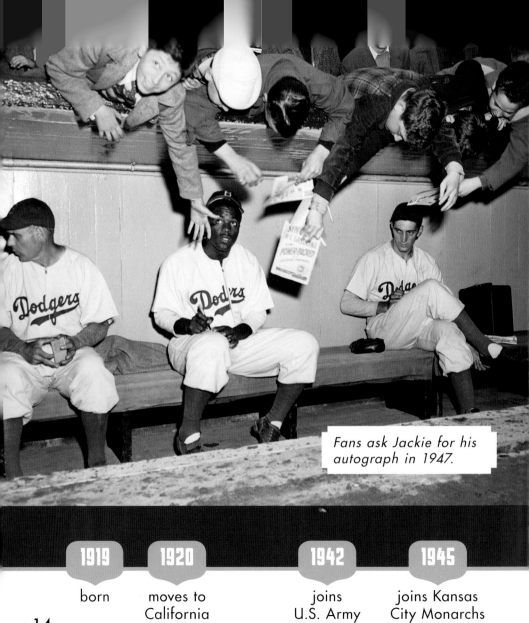

Fans ask Jackie for his autograph in 1947.

1919	1920	1942	1945
born	moves to California	joins U.S. Army	joins Kansas City Monarchs

In 1947 Jackie played

his first game with the

Brooklyn Dodgers.

He became the first

African-American player

in Major League Baseball.

1919	1920	1942	1945
born	moves to California	joins U.S. Army	joins Kansas City Monarchs

Players and fans did not

accept Jackie at first.

They yelled at him

on the baseball field.

But Jackie just kept

playing great baseball.

He became a hero.

1947

plays first game with
Brooklyn Dodgers

The Dodgers cheer after winning the World Series.

1919	1920		1942	1945
born	moves to California		joins U.S. Army	joins Kansas City Monarchs

Later Years

In 1955 Jackie and the Dodgers won the World Series. This is the biggest contest in baseball. In 1962 Jackie became the first African-American in the Baseball Hall of Fame.

1947
plays first game with
Brooklyn Dodgers

1955
Dodgers win
World Series

1962
enters Baseball
Hall of Fame

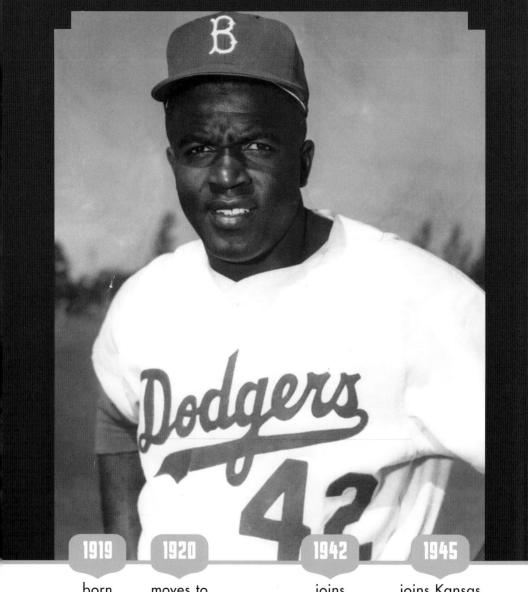

| 1919 | 1920 | | 1942 | 1945 |

born   moves to   joins   joins Kansas
California   U.S. Army   City Monarchs

Jackie died in 1972.

In 1997 he was given

a great honor. His number,

42, was retired. No Major

League player can ever

wear his number again.

1947	1955	1962	1972
plays first game with Brooklyn Dodgers	Dodgers win World Series	enters Baseball Hall of Fame	dies

Glossary

accept—to welcome someone into a group

college—a school that students attend after high school

contest—one or more games that people try to win

hall of fame—a place where important people are honored

hero—someone who has courage, strength, and does things that other people can't do

honor—an act of praise or respect

league—a group of sports teams that play against one another

Major League Baseball—the highest playing level of professional baseball

retire—to take something out of use

soldier—a person who is in the military

Read More

Fishman, Cathy Goldberg. *When Jackie and Hank Met.* Tarrytown, N.Y.: Marshall Cavendish, 2012.

McPherson, Stephanie Sammartino. *Jackie Robinson.* History Maker Bios. New York: Lerner, 2010.

Robinson, Sharon. *Jackie Robinson: American Hero.* New York: Scholastic, 2013.

Internet Sites

FactHound offers a safe, fun way to find Internet sites related to this book. All of the sites on FactHound have been researched by our staff.

Here's all you do:
Visit *www.facthound.com*
Type in this code: 9781491405024

Super-cool **stuff!**

Check out projects, games and lots more at
www.capstonekids.com

Critical Thinking Using the Common Core

1. How did Jackie act when people treated him poorly? Why do you think he did this? (Key Ideas and Details)

2. Look at the pictures on pages 8 and 16. What do these pictures tell you about Jackie as an athlete? (Craft and Structure)

Index

Word Count: 230
Grade: 1
Early-Intervention Level: 20